IEP *and* inclusion TIPS
for Parents and Teachers

TIPS

- Discuss IEPs with your child...

- Organize your child's records...

Anne I. Eason, Attorney-at-Law
Kathleen Whitbread, Ph.D.

IEP
RESOURCES

HANDOUT VERSION

Authors: Anne I. Eason and Kathy Whitbread

Editor: Tom Kinney

Graphic Design: Sherry Pribbenow

An Attainment Publication

P.O. Box 930160
Verona, Wisconsin 53593-0160

Phone 800-327-4269
Fax 800.942.3865

www.AttainmentCompany.com

ISBN 1-57861-573-9

About the Authors

Anne I. Eason, Esq.

Anne I. Eason is a special education attorney who limits her practice to inclusive education. She also trains parents and professionals about least restrictive environment for students with disabilities. You can read more about Anne's practice at www.spedlawyers.com.

Anne regularly teaches a 14 hour class on Understanding Special Education and has spoken at national conferences on inclusion. She is co-president, together with Beth Lurie, of SPED*NET, Special Education Network of New Canaan, Ltd. Anne maintains the SPED*NET website, www.spednet.org. The website received the 2004 Media of the Year award from the CT Coalition for Inclusive Education.

Anne graduated Hofstra University School of Law School in 1985, and is admitted to the NY, NJ, and CT bars. Prior to running a law practice, Anne was a social worker, working to get adults with disabilities successfully situated in the community during the era of closing institutions in the 1970's. Anne is the mother of four children. Her daughter Eva has Down syndrome and is fully and successfully included at New Canaan High School in New Canaan, CT.

Kathleen Whitbread, Ph.D.

Kathleen Whitbread is an Assistant Professor of Pediatrics and Associate Director of Programs for the University of Connecticut A. J. Pappanikou Center for Excellence in Developmental Disabilities Education, Research, and Service. Dr. Whitbread has over 20 years of experience in designing and managing programs in the fields of education and human services. As a former director of school and community services for a private, not-for-profit agency, she provided consultation and services to families, schools, and agencies on educational and behavioral supports for children with disabilities in typical settings. Dr. Whitbread has more than 15 years of experience as an educational consultant for children with disabilities being educated in inclusive classrooms. She has collaborated with educators in Russia, the Netherlands, Italy, and the United States to increase compliance with educational laws and improve the quality of education for children with disabilities in this country and abroad. Dr. Whitbread is the editor of The Inclusion Notebook, an award winning, internationally distributed publication of best practices in inclusive education. She is currently conducting research in the area of early literacy for children with intellectual disabilities and conducts preservice and inservice training in inclusive education, positive behavioral supports, and parent-professional partnerships.

Foreword

by Mary A. Falvey, Ph.D.

This manual was written by two very distinguished professionals, Attorney Anne Eason and Professor Kathleen Whitbread. Both Anne and Kathleen are also Moms who have made inclusion work for their children with disabilities and numerous other children with disabilities throughout their community.

What makes this manual on inclusive education so effective, are the practical tips based upon the authors own experiences as well as upon best practices delineated in the professional literature. As a parent myself, I found this manual so useful and parent friendly, I feel deeply it should be made available to all parents of school-aged children with disabilities.

The manual begins with a concise, but very comprehensive description of research related to and legislative history of inclusive education. This foundation provides parents with an understanding that inclusive education is not only a right that their sons and daughters have, but also the most effective service delivery model for students with disabilities.

"As a parent myself, I found this manual so useful and parent friendly; I feel deeply it should be made available to all parents of school aged children with disabilities."

Inclusive education, an approach used extensively in some communities and schools and only minimally available to others, is the most effective method for teaching students with disabilities. Inclusive education, when implemented with appropriate supports results in students with disabilities learning skills such as reading, writing, math, social interactions, communication and many other important skills (Falvey, 2005). In addition, students who do not have disabilities but go to school with students with disabilities, learn to interact with their peers who are different from them in some ways, but the same in other ways. They learn about compassion and empathy, two very important characteristics of well-adjusted and contributing adults.

This manual provides parents with systematic strategies they can use to become more active participants in the Individualized Education Plan (IEP) process and contribute to the development of a meaningful educational program for their sons and daughters. The strategies delineated in this manual are not expensive nor do they require that parents obtain degrees in education or advocacy in order to be effective. The strategies offer common sense approaches as to how to effectively advocate for inclusive education for their sons and daughters with disabilities.

Too often, professionals attending IEP meetings overwhelm parents with rules, regulations, and standardized assessment results. Professionals sometimes make the decisions about a student's goals and objectives and where he or she should go to school prior to the IEP meeting without ample input from the parents. As a result, parents are reluctant to offer their input since these critical decisions often have already been made. This manual provides parents with numerous strategies to ensure their input and build positive relationships with school professionals who work with their sons and daughters.

Chapters 1 and 2 provide very practical information on how parents can get prepared for their child's IEP meeting. The IEP is an important document since it drives services and supports necessary to make inclusion work for teachers and students alike. Numerous valuable tips are delineated in these two chapters that will assist in empowering parent to take a more active role in their child's IEP meeting.

Chapter 3, Ensuring Access to the General Education Curriculum describes an essential methodology required to make inclusion successful. It is not enough for students with disabilities to be physically included in general education classes; they must also be academically included. In order for academic inclusion to be successful, individualized supports, accommodations and adaptations must be provided to students based upon their needs (Falvey, 2005). This chapter includes an excellent delineation of these supports, accommodations, and adaptations.

Once a comprehensive and appropriate IEP is constructed with the genuine input of parents and students, the next step is to establish an appropriate method for systematically evaluating student progress over time. Assessment should not be about standardized test results that compare children to one another, but rather about painting a clear picture of a student so that appropriate supports and services can be made available to them and ongoing changes can be made based upon authentic assessment results. Chapter 4 provides parents with important information for evaluating student progress.

Having friends and being a friend are important roles for all children's development. Unfortunately, because of our traditional method of placing students with disabilities outside of their neighborhood schools, helping these students make friends and

"This book provides parents with important information for evaluating student progress.

It also provides wonderful tips for parent to help their children form and maintain friendships with their peers . . . and has many suggestions for what parents might do to contribute to the building of positive interactions and effective teams."

build friendship circles is negatively impacted by a segregated service delivery model (Falvey, 2005). Even students who attend their neighborhood schools sometimes experience difficulty in building and maintaining friendships. Chapter 5 provides wonderful tips for parent to help their children form and maintain friendships with their peers.

I have attended many team meetings, both IEP meetings as well as meetings for other purposes, sometimes as a friend of the student, sometimes as an advocate, sometimes as a teacher educator observing my student teachers participating in the meeting, sometimes as a parent, and sometimes as an aunt. Regardless of my role in these meetings, I have observed positive and negative interactions among and between the professionals and parents. The negative interactions have interfered with building positive educational outcomes for students with disabilities while the positive interactions generally yield positive educational outcomes because all the members of the team remained focused on the needs of the student rather than on their own egos. Teams of parents and educators who are committed to and use positive interaction styles are the most likely teams to be successful. Chapters 6 and 7 provide parents with numerous suggestions for what they might do to contribute to the building of positive interactions and effective teams. This chapter also includes sample notes and letters that parents can write to their child's teacher to foster the development of good communication and positive relationships.

Central to this book is the theme that parents are key to their children's success in school. If parents advocate for their sons and daughters throughout their schooling experiences, they will see them treated with respect and dignity while acquiring the skills necessary to be successful and building friendships with peers and others. If you use this book as a resource to help build your confidence and strength to advocate for your child's inclusion in their school and community, it will make an enormous difference in your child's life.

About Dr. Mary A. Falvey

Professor Mary Falvey is the director of Student Services in the Charter College of Education at California State University, Los Angeles (CSULA), where she oversees credential programs in elementary and secondary education, special education, educational administration, school counseling and school psychology. For 25 years, she was the coordinator of credentials and masters programs in Special Education at CSULA. She teaches courses in each of these programs as well as the doctoral program, which is a joint program with University of California, Los Angeles.

Dr. Falvey received her doctorate from the University of Wisconsin at Madison, her masters degree from San Francisco State University and her bachelors degree from Sacramento State University. A founding member of the California chapter of TASH and former member of the International TASH Board of Directors, Dr. Falvey has been a teacher and administrator of programs for students with and without disabilities, and has worked with numerous schools and school districts in developing inclusive educational services and programs. She is a consultant for numerous school districts on building inclusive educational practices. She has lectured at over 250 international, national, state, and local conferences as well as taught courses at numerous universities throughout the United States, Canada, Peru, and New Zealand. She has written, edited, and contributed chapters to over 14 books, and has recently published Believe in My Child with Special Needs: Helping Children Achieve Their Potential in School, through Paul H. Brookes Publishing Co., a book celebrating children's abilities and showing you how to secure for them the supports and services they need to be successful learners.

Dr. Falvey is the mother of two sons. One of her sons was identified as having a learning disability and received all his special education supports in his general education classes before graduating from high school. In addition, she has a nephew with Down syndrome who receives his special education supports within his general education classes. She is passionate about inclusive education and as a result has been instrumental in creating and supporting inclusive education for all of her family as well as numerous other families.

Mary A. Falvey, Ph.D.
Director of Student Services
Charter College of Education
California State University, Los Angeles
5151 State University Dr.
Los Angeles, CA 90032
(323)343-4320
mfalvey@calstatela.edu

Acknowledgements and Dedications

Kathleen Whitbread

I would like to thank Anne Eason, my co-author, friend, and colleague, for making this book a reality. And to C-PACE, my town's parent advocacy group, you are proof there is nothing more powerful than a group of moms with a cause. I'd like to also thank my husband Tom for supporting me in all that I do. I want to recognize my son Matthew's sensitivity to injustice and his willingness to speak up against it. Finally, I dedicate this book to my son Sam, whose sense of humor brightens my life, and whose fearless determination makes all my days an adventure.

Anne Eason

This book is first and foremost dedicated to my daughter Eva, whose very existence has defined all of my professional endeavors. I also dedicate this book to my three sons, Robbie, Karl, and Erik, who are disability advocates in their own right.

There are so many people to thank for making this book and my life's work possible. Thank you to my husband Bob, who never questions nor understands the pro bono work and volunteer efforts I am involved with; he just quietly pays all the bills. Thanks to my parents and siblings who always believed in my dreams. Thanks to all of the teachers and administrators that have touched Eva's life. Because they made a choice to fully and successfully include Eva, I was allowed to have a life beyond micromanaging my daughter's education. I want to thank Amy, Caitlin, Liz and Kat, who are wonderful friends with Eva, and never thought that Down syndrome was a barrier to friendship. Thanks to all of the advocates that came to meetings with me, including Kathy Whitbread, Michele Schneider, Eve Kessler, Paul Gaynor, and Beth Lurie, who spoke up for Eva when I was too emotionally involved to stay focused. Thanks to all the volunteers who help organize our parent group, SPED*NET New Canaan, including Beth Lurie, Victoria Muñoz, Debbie Simpson and now Judi Anders, and all the countless professionals who paraded in every month, volunteering to speak to our parents over the years. Parents need to stand on each other's shoulders in order to insure good programs for their kids. Our parent group worked collaboratively with the New Canaan Public Schools, thanks to our Special Education Director, Dr. Candy Lombardo, and other staff who believed that parents were equal and important partners with the educational process. Thanks to all of the folks who support my law practice. My colleague and friend, special education attorney Nora Belanger, with whom I share an office suite, who is always available to discuss cases, share legal resources, and grab a cappuccino with me when I need a break. I can't even imagine running a practice without checking in with her every day. Thanks also to all of my clients who made the decision that inclusion was not negotiable. I am privileged to be a part of their successes. Thanks to my coauthor, Dr. Kathleen Whitbread, without whom this book would have been impossible. She's been a friend and mentor for many years. Thanks also to Tom Kinney, our editor, who believed in our project and has been fun and interesting to work with.

If I was to thank each person who has helped me walk on my journey, this acknowledgement would be longer than the book! Life has been good.

What Does the Research Say About Inclusive Education?

by Kathleen Whitbread, Ph.D.

The Civil Rights movement of the 1950s and 1960s was a precursor to legislation protecting the rights of children with disabilities to a public education. In the Supreme Court ruling of Brown vs. Board of Education in 1954, Chief Justice Earl Warren, referring to segregation of children by race, stated:

Today, education is perhaps the most important function of state and local governments . . . it is a principal instrument in awakening the child to cultural values, in preparing him for later professional training, and in helping him to adjust normally to his environment. In these days, it is doubtful that any child may reasonably be expected to succeed in life if he is denied the opportunity of an education. Such an opportunity . . . is a right which must be made available on equal terms. We conclude that in the field of education, the doctrine "separate and equal" has no place (Brown v. Broard of Education, 1954).

These same arguments, originally applied to race, have been repeated on behalf of children with disabilities, many of whom continue to be educated separately from their nondisabled peers despite legislation mandating otherwise (U.S. Department of Education, 2003).

There is a strong research base to support the education of children with disabilities alongside their nondisabled peers. Although separate classes, with lower student to teacher ratios, controlled environments and specially trained staff would seem to offer benefits to a child with a disability, research fails to demonstrate the effectiveness of such programs (Lipsky, 1997; Sailor, 2003). There is mounting evidence that, other than a smaller class size, "there is little that is special about the special education system," and that the negative effects of separating children with disabilities from their peers far outweigh any benefit to smaller classes (Audette & Algozzine, 1997).

Students with disabilities in inclusive classrooms show academic gains in a number of areas, including improved performance on standardized tests, mastery of IEP goals, grades, on-task behavior and motivation to learn (National Center for Education Restructuring and Inclusion, 1995). Moreover, placement in inclusive classrooms

> *"There is a strong research base to support the education of children with disabilities alongside their nondisabled peers.*
>
> *Students with disabilities in inclusive classrooms show academic gains in a number of areas."*

does not interfere with the academic performance of students without disabilities with respect to the amount of allocated time and engaged instructional time, the rate of interruption to planned activities and student achievement on test scores and report card grades (York, Vandercook, MacDonald, Heise-Neff, and Caughey, 1992).

The types of instructional strategies found in inclusive classrooms, including peer tutoring, cooperative learning groups and differentiated instruction, have been shown to be beneficial to all learners. For example, Slavin, Madden, & Leavy (1984) found that math scores for students with and without disabilities increased by nearly half a grade level as a result of working in cooperative learning groups. Peer tutoring resulted in significant increases in spelling, social studies and other academic areas for students with and without disabilities (Maheady et al, 1988; Pomerantz et al, 1994). The use of graphic organizers, study guides, and computer accommodations resulted in significantly improved performances on tests and quizzes for students with and without disabilities (Horton, Lovitt, & Berglund, 1990). In addition, children with intellectual disabilities educated in general education settings have been found to score higher on literacy measures than students educated in segregated settings (Buckley, 2000).

Quality inclusive education doesn't just happen. Educating children with disabilities in general education settings with access to the general education environment requires careful planning and preparation (Deno, 1997; King-Spears, 1997; Scott, Vitale, & Masten, 1998). Research shows that principals, special education directors, superintendents, teachers, parents and community members must all be involved and invested in the successful outcome of inclusive education (Villa, 1997; Walther-Thomas, 1997). Teachers — both general and special education — must collaborate to create learning strategies and environments that work for all students. Related service personnel, including speech therapists, occupational therapists, physical therapists and school psychologists will be expected to deliver their services in the general education environment rather than in pull-out rooms and will need to incorporate their services into the general education curriculum and schedule (Ferguson, Ralph, & Katul, 1998). Educators must rethink assessment, as No Child Left Behind and IDEA 2004 both call for more extensive evaluation of student progress, including the use of standardized assessment.

Research highlights the benefits of efforts on the part of schools to find meaningful and creative ways for parents of children with disabilities to participate and contribute in the school community (Ryndak & Downing, 1996.) The benefits of strong family-school partnerships are well documented in the literature. Student academic achievement is higher when parents are involved; in fact, the higher the level of parent involvement, the higher the level of student achievement (Dauber & Epstein, 1993; Henderson & Berla, 1994; Christenson & Sheridan, 2001). Other benefits of strong family-school collaboration include improved student attendance, higher aspirations for postsecondary education and career development (Caplan, et. al., 1997), improved social competence, (Webster-Stratton, 1993) and lower rates of high-risk behavior on the part of adolescents (Resnick et al., 1997).

The Individuals with Disabilities Education Act (IDEA) strongly emphasizes the involvement of families at every step of the special education process, from referral to evaluation, to Individualized Education Program (IEP) development, to monitoring progress. Yet, many parents of students with disabilities are not fully participating members of their child's IEP Team. Data from the first year of the Special Education Elementary Longitudinal Study (SEELS) funded by the Office of Special Education Programs (OSEP) as part of the national assessment of the 1997 Individuals with Disabilities Education Act (IDEA 97), showed that:

• Nearly 90 percent of elementary and middle school students with disabilities had a family member attend their IEP meeting but only two-thirds of parents reported collaborating with school district personnel on the IEP development.

• Parents of students with specific learning disabilities and speech/ language impairment were the least likely to attend IEP meetings or training sessions. Since these two disability categories comprise 70 percent of all students (ages 6-21) served under IDEA, the SEELS study implies that the majority of students with disabilities have the least involved families.

• Only 25 percent of students had an adult family member who had participated in an informational or training session on understanding their rights and responsibilities under IDEA. Those who attended viewed the meetings as very helpful (49%) or somewhat helpful (44%).

"Student academic achievement is higher when parents are involved; in fact, the higher the level of parent involvement, the higher the level of student achievement."

A national survey by Public Agenda, When Its Your Child: A Report on Special Education from the Families Who Use It, revealed that a large majority (70%) of the parents surveyed say that too many children with special needs lose out because their parents don't know what's available to them. More than half (55%) said that parents have to find out on their own what services and supports are available. This finding underscores the need to provide more training and information to parents on how the special education process works and their rights under IDEA.

A lack of information about the special education process can lead to conflicts between parents and schools. In studies of conflict resolution in special education, breakdowns of communication between parents and schools were often caused by "parents not being adequately informed as to what limits are contained in IDEA and School district personnel not being adequately informed about the extent and complexity of the . . . federal statues and regulations" (Feinberg, et al. 2002).

"Nearly 90 percent of elementary and middle school students with disabilities had a family member attend their IEP meeting but only two-thirds of parents reported collaborating with School district personnel on the IEP development."

This book is our attempt to provide parents with tips and strategies for making inclusive education a reality for their children. It is our hope that these tips will prove useful for families as they advocate for their children, and will allow parents to come to the IEP table as true and equal partners in the IEP process.

Chapter 1

Getting Prepared for the IEP Meeting

Productive and successful IEP meetings require careful preparation on the part of all team members. Parents who arrive at their child's IEP meeting without doing their homework risk leaving the meeting without a full understanding of what they agreed to, or worse, having agreed to things they feel are not in the best interests of their child. In order to participate fully and confidently in the IEP meeting, parents must be educated about the process, be familiar with all the key players, and in possession of all the information needed to make knowledgeable decisions about their child.

"*In the middle of difficulty lies opportunity.*"

Albert Einstein

"*Before anything else, preparation is the key to success.*"

Alexander Graham Bell

1 Communicate with your child. Ask how school is going. Ask your child what he or she would like to change, what they would like to be different in school. Find out what they like and dislike. Ask them what they want and what they need.

Not all children with disabilities are verbal. If necessary, alternative means of communication are available and should be accessed.

2 Be prepared to share relevant information about your child with the team. Consider putting together a portfolio of your child's home experiences, including photos or videos of your child engaging in family life and activities.

3 Be sure to write down any questions you may have before the meeting so you do not forget. These questions can be part of a written agenda you submit to the school before the meeting.

4 Call or make an appointment to introduce yourself to each of your child's teachers. Don't forget the "specials" teachers (art, music, physical education, etc.) and related services staff (occupational therapist, speech therapist, physical therapist, etc.). Find out from them how they think your child is doing at school, what their concerns are, and what help or resources they may need to do their job. Ask them to share their vision for your child for next year.

5 Visit your child's classroom. Visit the cafeteria during lunch, visit the playground to see what happens at recess. Observe what's going on with your child in all settings while they are at school (but don't overstay your welcome and respect the teacher's space).

6 Organize all records pertaining to your child. It is helpful to put records in a three-ring binder, arranged either chronologically, or by section (evaluations, IEPs, report cards, etc).

Some people like to put the most recent information on top. I like putting it on the bottom, so my records read like a book, especially if you are putting the records in a binder. — Anne

7 Keep good records of all communication in connection with your child. After each telephone call or meeting, write down everything that was said, creating a contemporaneous business record. Get into the habit of documenting each important conversation with a follow-up letter but respect each teacher's busy schedule. Don't burden them with unnecessary contacts.

8 Review last year's records and the current IEP.

9 Do you have all the information you need about your child?

Read all of the prior evaluations. Decide if additional evaluations are needed and how that information will be obtained. Do you fully understand your child's diagnosis? Do you understand the words used in the reports? Don't be afraid to ask someone to explain any jargon. Get a written copy of the results of any assessments. If needed, schedule a meeting with the appropriate school personnel to discuss assessment results.

10 Bring in any evaluations that were done privately if you want the school team to consider them. Make sure they have copies at least 5 days in advance of the meeting so they have time to review them. Remember, by law, the team only has to consider the evaluation, not follow the recommendations.

11 If you disagree with the school's evaluation, you may request (in writing) an independent educational evaluation at the district's expense. The district is required to pay for the evaluation unless they are willing to bring you to a due process hearing to prove that their evaluation was appropriate.

12 Prior to the IEP meeting, let the school know in writing what you will be recommending for your child. Send in a proposed agenda. Be clear on what your expectations are. Bring documentation of what your child needs to be successful in school.

13 Check to see who has been invited to the IEP. Is everyone who is important to your child's educational program going to be there? Is everyone who is legally required to be there planning to attend? Think carefully before you allow someone to be excused. Check the law to see who is required to be at the meeting. Let the school know if you are planning to bring someone to the meeting.

14 Know your rights. Download or write for a free copy of the IDEA and read it. Visit the web sites for the US Department of Education as well as your State Department of Education (SDE). Sign up for training to learn about your legal rights. Become empowered with knowledge.

"*Two roads diverged in a wood and I took the one less traveled by, and that has made all the difference.*"

Robert Frost

Familiarize yourself with the laws regarding special education. You can obtain free copies of IDEA from the US Dept of Education and a copy of your state's special education regulations from your SDE. If you don't understand the law, call the SDE and speak to a representative. There are consultants who can answer your questions and explain the process in straightforward terms.

15 Speak with other parents about their IEP meetings. Ask them if they will share their experiences. Get their impressions (both positive and negative) of the services they received. Participate in local parent groups so you have a network of parents to rely on. You will benefit from hearing about other parents' experiences.

16 Consider placement in regular education for your child. A regular class placement, commonly called "inclusion," is defined by Office of Special Education Programs as 80% or more of the day in a regular class. Don't be afraid to insist that this be considered. The law says that to the maximum extent appropriate, children with disabilities shall be educated in their neighborhood schools and attend regular classes (the classes he or she would have attended if born without a disability) with supplemental aids and services necessary for success. There is ample research to show that inclusion is good for all kids — with and without disabilities. Make the commitment and decide what supports your child needs to be successful. It is never too late to start.

"*Speak with other parents about their IEP meetings. Get their impressions (both positive and negative).*"

March 9, 2005

Mr. Sigmund Freud, School Psychologist
My Middle School
New Canaan, CT 06840

Re: FERPA Request for all of Ivy Smith's records

Dear Mr. Freud,

     In preparation for Ivy's upcoming IEP, I am requesting a copy of all of her records since she began kindergarten in September 1999. I am entitled to these records under FERPA, The Family Education Rights and Privacy Act, and IDEA.

     Please include all of her records, which include but are not limited to: Her cumulative file, her confidential file, and her compliance file. Include all records generated by the school, as well as records that came to school with Ivy, and any records sent to the school or obtained from any source. Please include all reports written as a result of the school's evaluations; reports of independent evaluations; medical records; summary reports of evaluation team and eligibility committee meetings; IEP's; any correspondence retained between myself and the school officials; any correspondence written between school personnel regarding my daughter; any records maintained by the school nurse, Ivy's teachers, and any member of the IEP team; notes or letters written in connection with any planning or discussions, or any other matters in connection with my daughter Ivy Smith. Please include any and all personally identifiable information that exists.

     Thanks in advance for your cooperation.

Very truly yours,

Anne Smith

123 Main Street
New Canaan, CT 06840

Tel: (203) 966-1234
Fax: (203) 966-5678
Smith55@aol.com

Sample letter

17 Write a letter to get copies of all of your child's records prior to the IEP meeting. Parents must have as much information about their child as is possible in order to be full participants in the IEP process; their participation must be meaningful. You have a right to this information under IDEA as well as under FERPA (Family Education Rights and Privacy Act).

FERPA provides access to the records not necessarily a "copy" of them. Clarify with your school district first.

18 Create a vision statement for your child. Don't be afraid to dream. Having a big picture in your mind will help put small pieces in place.

Notes

The IEP
Tips for What to do During the IEP Meeting

The Individualized Education Program (IEP) has been referred to as "the cornerstone" or "centerpiece" of the Individuals with Disabilities Education Act (IDEA). It is the statutory vehicle for ensuring that a student with a disability receives a free appropriate public education in the least restrictive environment.

The IEP is an individualized document, written for each student, memorializing the educational program that is designed to meet each child's unique needs. All students who receive special education services must have an IEP. The IEP is developed during an IEP meeting with the full participation of the parents and the student, when he or she is old enough to contribute.

"The IEP is an individualized document, written for each student, memorializing the educational program that is designed to meet each child's unique needs."

19 Consider sitting at the head of the table where you can project confidence. In order to get the best seat, you must arrive early.

This "take charge" style isn't for every parent. Follow your inner voice and find your own way to participate fully in the IEP meeting.

20 Send your agenda to the district a few days ahead of time. Label it "Proposed Agenda." Bring extra copies to the meeting and politely invite team members to take one.

21 Bring food, or at least bottled water. If your water bottles are large, bring a stack of cups. At the end of the meeting, leave the food for the staff to enjoy. Use plastic or paper plates and trays; avoid plates that you would want to bring home.

I used to bring in home-baked muffins or cookies, but these days everyone seems to be on a diet. You never know if they are counting calories, trying to eat low fat food, or counting carbs. Now I just bring water, both flat and sparkling, with an assortment of flavors. It's appreciated and doesn't make a mess of the meeting area. But, homemade goodies are always a good option. Dieters don't have to indulge if they don't choose to.
— Anne

22 You are a full and equal member of the IEP team. Don't be afraid to take charge and see yourself as equally important to professionals. Do not allow yourself to get into a "them versus me" situation. Also, be sure that every time someone says, "The team feels . . ." you also agree with the statement. If you do not, say, "I don't feel that way and I am a full and equal member of this team." Remember that you have a valuable and unique perspective as the parent of your child.

23 Be an active listener. Make sure you make eye contact with people as they are speaking. Give each speaker your full attention. Allow people to finish their thoughts before speaking up. Don't fidget.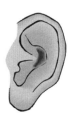

24 If the school did not provide records on evaluations ahead of time and you feel your ability to participate in the meeting has been compromised, consider adjourning the meeting (with the utmost of tact and class) until you can review the reports. The law says that parents are fully participating members of the IEP and you cannot be a fully participating member if you lack critical information about your child.

25 Discuss the issues your child has that may affect his ability to receive educational benefits in the general education environment. Focus on what supports and services your child may need to be successful. For example, "Due to Tim's hearing impairment, he requires a sign language interpreter to benefit from the general education curriculum." Requests should be appropriate.

26 Ask ahead of time that no reports or evaluations be read or produced for the first time at the meeting. Write to the school and ask if all reports, evaluations and proposed goals and objectives can be given to you at least 5 days ahead of time so you can be prepared to contribute to the IEP discussion in a meaningful way. Exchanging information ahead of time gives all parties an opportunity to become better prepared. It also leads to more efficient use of time at the meetings.

27 In the corporate world, business goals are SMART, which means specific, measurable, action oriented, realistic, and time measurable. Make sure your IEP goals are SMART as well.

Note: This excellent advice originates from the corporate world by way of the good people at wrightslaw.com

28 Be sure you understand the "prior written notice" provision in IDEA. IDEA says that notice must be given whenever the school proposes to initiate a change or refuses to make a change in connection with: The identification, evaluation, or educational placement of the child, or the provision of FAPE (free appropriate public education) to the child. This notice must include a description of the action proposed or refused by the agency; an explanation of why the agency proposes or refuses to take the action, a description of any other options that the agency considered and the reasons why those options were rejected; a description of each evaluation procedure, test, record, or report the agency used as a basis for the proposed or refused action; a description of any other factors that are relevant to the agency's proposal or refusal; a statement that the parents of a child with a disability have protection under the procedural safeguards of this part and, if this notice is not an initial referral for evaluation, the means by which a copy of a description of the procedural safeguards can be obtained; and sources for parents to contact to obtain assistance in understanding the provisions of this part.

29 If you don't understand what is being said, ask for clarification.

30 Do not permit a discussion of placement until the present level of performance has been discussed and then the goals and objectives. The law that placement is discussed only after the IEP goals and objectives have been developed.

31 Bring your child to the IEP meeting. If you feel it is inappropriate for her to stay for the entire meeting, bring her for part of the meeting.

Notes:

If you are curious as to what happens to a boy who goes to his sister's IEP meetings . . . this is how the story unfolds. In an effort to continue advocacy training, I brought my son to a disability related rally in Washington, DC. He knew the

32 Consider bringing all your children to the IEP meeting so they can support their sibling.

33 Consider inviting other students to the IEP meeting. Kids often have great ideas on how to support students. Of course, your child needs to be okay with this.

Why did I bring Eva's brothers to her IEP meeting beginning in the second grade? Did they understand the meeting? Well . . . not entirely. However, they knew I was always attending meetings and I wanted to take away some of the mystery. Also, I wanted my sons to see how I advocated for my daughter. I wanted them to witness how one individual could stand up for an idea, even if everyone in the room disagreed. I am preparing them to grow up and hopefully become co-advocates with their sister, who I am grooming to become a self-advocate. It's okay with me if they attend the IEP meeting to escape going to science. It's okay with me if they attend the IEP meeting just because I am feeding them chocolate milk and bagels.
— Anne

34 Try not to go to an IEP alone. The person you bring does not necessarily have to be a trained advocate, they can be someone who cares about your child and family. If necessary, ask them not to speak. Just having them there, writing notes, will let the district know that you take your rights seriously.

purpose of the rally, but admittedly I had to sell it as a day off of school with some sightseeing. He agreed to go, knowing that the rally piece was something he had to put up with. Look and see how transformations occur!

Tips on Advocates

- When you choose an advocate, make sure that he or she is prepared.
- Make sure the person presents him or herself in a professional manner.
- Make sure that the advocate shares your views on inclusive education.
- Some advocates bring their own anger to the table. Choose someone who is diplomatic but strong.
- Do not forego preparation for the IEP meeting because you "trust" your advocate.
- Prepare for the meeting WITH your advocate. They must represent your point of view; they are not there to take over. This is YOUR child and YOUR meeting.
- When preparing with your advocate, identify what is not negotiable, and what you are willing to compromise on. Prioritize your issues.
- Make sure your advocate has a copy of and has read all of your child's records.
- Do not hire an advocate 1 day before the meeting. The advocate will not have enough time to read the records and prepare properly with you.

35 If your school district allows it, tape record your IEP meeting. You will have a completely accurate record of the meeting and you will be free to listen and participate in the meeting rather than writing notes. Note, however, the district cannot refuse to allow you to tape if it's an accommodation for the parent, for example if the parent is hearing impaired.

"When one door of happiness closes, another opens; but often we look so long at the closed door that we do not see the one which has opened for us."

Helen Keller

Tips on Taping!

Note: Check with your district. It's up to them whether or not you can tape.

- Let the school know ahead of time that you will be taping. Most schools will want to have their own tape recorder running too and this gives them notice that they will need to have a recorder and tapes.

- Get a tote bag to hold your tape recorder with fresh batteries. Then bring extra batteries and extra tapes. The tape packages should already be opened so you are not fumbling around trying to get the wrapper off. Have the labels already marked. Otherwise, you may start taping over your own tape. Mark the labels Ivy Smith's IEP, date, tape one of ___. Start with fresh batteries, and bring extras. Also bring an extra tape recorder. I have seen meetings stopped because the school could not find their own tape recorder. Don't rely on a cord, there may not be an empty outlet. Also, the cord might be too short, and you don't want to create a distraction by using a big extension cord.

- Use a regular sized cassette recorder and not the microcassette recorder. Small microcassettes do not produce the same quality sound and they are not as sensitive as full size cassette tapes.

- Don't buy low end blank tapes. These cheaper tapes will stretch more easily especially when they are in fast forwarded or rewound.

- Make sure your recorder makes a noise when it shuts off. You don't want to have the meeting running if the tape has stopped, nor do you want to watch the clock to guess how much more time you have. Buy the longest playing tapes to avoid switching often. You can also consider bringing someone to the meeting whose job it will be to watch the tape, and turn it to the other side when necessary. You might forget to do it.

- Make sure the tape has a good microphone — an external mike is usually best. If you choose a tape recorder with the built-in microphone, there may be too much noise (rumbling sound) transmitted from the motor which drives the cassette to the microphone.

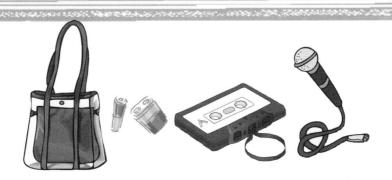

- Point the external mike up towards the ceiling, so sounds from all around the room will be picked up. If the mike is self powered, make sure the battery is fresh.

- Don't keep the tape recorder next to you. Put it in the middle of the table. Place the tape recorder on a book or pad. Often the tape motor creates a slight rumbling that can affect the microphone.

- When the meeting is over, do not immediately turn the tape recorder off. Keep it running. Critical details are often discussed after the IEP meeting is over.

- When you are home, break the tabs to prevent someone from taping over the tape.

- Listen to the tape! You'll be surprised at how much you have missed!

- If you are going to be involved in a due process hearing, have all of your IEP meeting tapes transcribed. You can do this yourself, or hire a professional transcriber. If you transcribe the tape on your own, double space and always state who is speaking. Number the pages. If you use the tape at a hearing, submit the tape with the transcription. The tape will be your evidence, the transcription will be an aid to understanding the tape. (FERPA, the Family Educational Rights and Privacy Act ("FERPA"; 20 U.S.C. 1232g), and is subject to the confidentiality requirements of the regulations.)

- Consider the new technology! *For example, digital voice recorder/music players are sleek and fun to use. They record directly into internal memory or use a removable memory card. Then the recording can be played back, or uploaded directly to your computer and sent electronically to others or kept as a record until you are ready to access the info. The recorders come with USB connectivity for high speed copying of files to a PC. Recently, I have been to IEPs where Mom whips out her child's iPod and records the meeting! There's an accessory that allows you to do that, at this time only for the full-sized iPods. If you buy a digital recorder, make sure it can record for as long as your IEP lasts. Also make sure it can upload to your computer. Before you use it, make sure you are familiar with the technology.*
— Anne

36 Always debrief with your advocate, spouse, or whoever accompanied you immediately after the meeting. Write down what you remember, and then add your own opinions. Then write a thank you note for the time people spent meeting about your child. Use the note to document key decisions and to review the issues that are still unresolved.

"*The best way to predict your future is to create it.*"

Anonymous

Creating Legally Correct and Usable IEPs

37 Insure that each proposed goal is measurable and is based on your child's evaluations.

38 Determine the criteria that will be used to evaluate whether or not goals were met. These criteria must be completely clear and understandable to all team members, including you. If the team recommends a criteria of "80% or more," ask that this be explained. Is it that the child will perform the task correctly 80% of the school day? Or is the child going to perform 80% of the task correctly every day? Or is the child going to perform the task correctly 4 out of 5 days of the week? Or will the child perform the task 80% of the time in any given hour that data are collected? This needs to be crystal clear to every team member since this is the measure that will be used to determine if the child has successfully acquired a skill.

39 If behavior impedes learning, make sure that a positive behavior plan is put in place. A positive behavior plan is based on a "functional behavior analysis," which is a way of looking at the causes of behavior as well as the aspects of a child's learning environment that may be contributing to the behavior.

40 The IEP must clearly and specifically state where services are to take place. Do not agree to "in the classroom OR in the resource room, as appropriate." This will leave the decision of where to provide services up to the therapist or implementer, and leaves the door open for the service to be provided where it is more convenient for staff, rather than what is best for the child.

41 Consider asking for support for the teacher and other staff members that work with your child. The law allows you to request services that are provided to the parents or teachers of a child with a disability to help them to more effectively work with him or her. This might include training about the specific disability to allow the teacher to work more effectively to include and educate your child.

42 Consider asking for support for you as a parent to work with your child. The law allows for parent counseling and training to assist you in understanding the individual needs of your child, to provide you with information about child development and help to acquire the necessary skills to support the implementation of your child's IEP or IFSP.

43 Remember that test results are not always reliable. They are merely a snapshot of a certain moment of time in your child's life.

44 Consider how related services can be integrated within the school day and not become a pull-out service. Embedding related services into typical routines offers the opportunity for the student to practice the skill in the setting where they will be expected to demonstrate it.

Related Services

Related services include transportation and such developmental, corrective, and other supportive services required to assist a child with a disability to benefit from special education. The evaluation process helps the team determine what related services the student needs. We recommend that you think ahead about how related services can be provided in the general education environment. For example, if the speech teacher wants to facilitate pragmatic language skills, couldn't that be done over lunchtime in the cafeteria? Not a "lunch bunch" with 6 students, all receiving special education services, but a typical lunch group with the speech therapist seated near by. Articulation goals can be met during a foreign language class, when everyone is struggling with new words. And what about physical therapy? Should students practice going up and down stairs that lead nowhere in order to perfect alternating feet movements? Ask the PT to meet the student in the hallways when the student is going upstairs for a reason. Or the PT could meet the student at recess or during gym and work on skills, to avoid always relying on the "pull-out" model. Don't think related services is something a therapist can only do with a student in a private room and then hope the skills transfer over. It's not just an effort to "fix" a child by doing related services three times a week for 20 minutes. Related services can be taught in natural environments, empowering students to do real things in real settings. Look across all of the school settings. Think of how related services personnel can help students in places that they already are in.

45 Plan for recreational activities to promote social inclusion and to help the student make friends.

46 Consider assistive technology. The law requires that a discussion of assistive technology needs be conducted for every child as part of their IEP.

47 Classes with a disproportionate number of students with disabilities, sometimes called "transitional classes" or reverse mainstream classes, are not inclusive classes. These are special education placements. You may or may not want this for your child. If you want your child in a regular class placement, do not agree to a class with a disproportionate number of children with disabilities. Inclusive classes follow the law of natural proportions, whereby the school and classroom reflect the community at large. If there are 10% of the people in your community who have disabilities, then the classroom should contain no more that 10% of the students with disabilities.

48 If your child will eventually transition out of public schools, consider post secondary school options. Even kids with significant cognitive disabilities can attend colleges. College courses can be modified and accommodations can be offered. Section 504 of the Rehabilitation Act of 1974 and the Americans with Disabilities Act (ADA) will offer legal protections and moral guidance. If your child attends the graduation ceremony with his classmates but does not get a diploma, the public school district can support him in a post secondary option.

49 Insure that the role of the paraprofessional for your child is clear. Make sure that a good plan is in place so the paraprofessional does not become your child's "private teacher, teaching your child while the classroom teacher instructs the rest of the class. Clarify the roles of each adult in the classroom. Make sure the teacher has established a method to communicate his or her daily expectations and lesson plans for the entire class.

The Power of Vision!

"*The ability to see beyond our present reality, to create, to invent what does not yet exist, to become what we not yet are. It gives us the capacity to live out of our imagination instead of our memory.*"

Steven Covey

50 If a student uses augmentative or alternative communication (AAC), make sure the communication system is always readily available. If someone needs to assist the student, make sure other students, not only the teacher, can assist. Make sure the entire school gets the opportunity to be involved with the AAC. When a teacher communicates with the student, it should be in a respectful manner so the teacher can serve as a role model to other students.

51 Remember, the 'I' in IEP stands for INDIVIDUAL. Write an IEP that is individually tailored to your child's strengths and needs. Do not allow the school to pick from a menu and give you a McIEP. The IEP must be individualized, specially designed, to meet the unique educational needs of each student.

52 Ask your child what she wants in her IEP. Believe in her. Encourage her to make choices and take control.

Thinking About Evaluations

53 The purpose of an evaluation is either to determine if a student is eligible for special education services or to provide useful information to the general education teacher on how to effectively teach that student in the general education environment. It is not simply to generate numbers or scores.

"*Far away, there in the sunshine are my highest aspirations. I may not reach them, but I can look up and see their beauty, believe in them, and try to follow where they lead.*"

Louisa May Alcott

Tips on Planning an Evaluation

• Be sure you are comfortable with all tests or evaluations recommended for your child. The law requires that you sign a release for all evaluations. Speak to your pediatrician, a representative of a parent group, or an advocacy organization about tests recommended for your child so you are both knowledgeable and comfortable with the evaluation process.

• In some instances, you may opt to arrange for a private evaluator rather than consent to the school district's evaluator administering a particular test or assessment. Some reasons parents may choose this option include:

When you want to control what information is included in your child's permanent school file — some psychological testing may include a detailed family history and you may wish to keep information not directly related to your child's education out of her school record.

When you are not confident that the proposed test will be an accurate measure of your child's ability — some intelligence testing does not capture the true abilities of children who are non verbal or who have difficulty communicating. You may wish to choose an evaluator who is skilled in administering non-verbal IQ tests.

When you are not confident in the training or skill of the evaluator — Many parents mistakenly assume that all school psychologists are Ph.D. level practitioners or that all Occupational Therapists have been trained in sensory integration techniques. This is not necessarily true. You may wish to choose an evaluator whose skill or training exceeds the minimum qualifications of school district personnel.

• Keep in mind that if you choose to bypass the school evaluator in favor of a private evaluator, you will be responsible for paying for the evaluation. It is important to share relevant data with the IEP team for use in planning your child's program.

"The most damaging phrase in language is: "It's always been done that way."

Alexander Graham Bell

Making Placement Decisions

54 When deciding on placement, the first consideration for every single child should the general education curriculum in the school and classroom they would attend if they had been born without a disability. Make sure that the correct sequence of steps is followed in deciding on placement. Placement decisions shouldn't:

> a. Be made based on a child's label ("Paul has cerebral palsy so he'll go to Room 5 where all the kids with CP go").
>
> b. Be made before the IEP is developed.
>
> c. Be based on administrative convenience (for example, because all the special education teachers and related personnel are located in one school).

55 Placement decisions should ALWAYS:

> d. Be made by the IEP team, not one or two members of the team.
>
> e. Be reviewed at least annually.
>
> f. Be made based on the educational needs of the child.

"*If we are to achieve a richer culture . . . we must weave one in which each diverse human gift will find a fitting place.*"

Margaret Mead

Notes

Chapter 3

Ensuring Access to the General Education Curriculum

Almost 30 years of research and experience has demonstrated that the education of children with disabilities can be made more effective by . . . having high expectations for such children and ensuring their access to the general education curriculum in the regular classroom, to the maximum extent possible . . . Individuals with Disabilities Education Improvement Act of 2004, Section 601.

Ensuring access to the general education curriculum means providing students with disabilities access to the same curriculum and educational environment as that provided to all students. Successful access results from the implementation of appropriate supports, strategies, services, and validated programs and practices. Access to the general education curriculum, by students with disabilities, is legally mandated by IDEA.

"I have learned that in order to bring about change, one must take the first step, or else it will not be done."

Rosa Parks

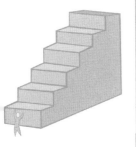

Curriculum Design and Modification

56 Start out by asking if the student can do the lesson the same way as the rest of the class. Don't assume that every lesson will need to be modified.

(Editor's Note: Modifications are done by the teaching staff. The information presented here is to help you understand how they work so you can better advocate for your child.)

57 Only use one-to-one adult assistance if you have already tried less restrictive supports, such as small group learning, peer tutoring, augmentative communication, picture schedules, and so on.

58 Build collaboration time between special education and regular education personnel into the IEP to be sure there is time to adequately plan modifications.

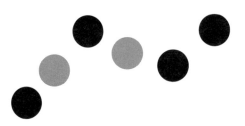

59 Use picture schedules for young children to avoid dependence on adults to alert them to what is coming next.

60 To begin to teach independent organizational skills, color code loose papers in middle schoolers' planners by subject. For example, all science papers have a red dot on the top, social studies papers have a green dot, and so on so that the student can independently file and organize their planner.

61 Teach problem solving skills to children so they can participate in modifying lessons for diverse groups. For example, have small groups of students brainstorm as many ways as possible to teach a lesson.

62 Keep good records of modified lessons so they are available for you to draw on when working with other students who may have similar learning needs.

63 When modifying students work, be sure to maintain the core idea of the lesson. For example, if you are reading a story, assigning only some of the pages would prevent the student from answering comprehension questions related to the entire story. Try books on tape or scanned text so the student learns the most important content.

64 Follow a continuum when modifying work.

Some Examples:

Can the student do what the rest of the class is doing?
If not, then determine the following:

- Can the student be given extra cues or prompts (such as highlighted text, or verbal prompts from teacher) to accomplish the goals of the lesson? If not, then:

- Can the student get assistance from a peer to complete the lesson? If not, then:

- Can the student work in a cooperative learning group with adult assistance? If not, then:

- Can the student work on the same lesson with direct adult assistance? If not then:

- Can the student work on a modified version of the lesson, accomplishing the most important objectives of the lesson? If not, then:

- Can the student work on an alternate activity that accomplishes the goals of the lesson? And so on.

65 Use the principles of universal design to create plans that will meet the needs of a diverse group of students. Universal design is the design of activities and environments to be usable by all students, to the greatest extent possible, without the need for adaptation or modification. For example, for all literature lessons, have stories available in print, on tape, in scanned computerized text, in large print text, Braille, with additional pictures to accompany the text, a video or movie of the story, a script to act out the story, and with text available at a variety of grade levels. This way you won't have to "reinvent the wheel" every time a student enters your class with specialized learning needs.

66 Pay attention to the environment. Some children may need to move around more than other children, or may need quiet space to work without distractions. Also consider special seating, study carrels, providing space for movement or breaks or providing help to organize work space.

Key Concept:

*"Universal Design is the design of activities
and environments to be usable by all students,
to the greatest extent possible, without the
need for adaptation or modification."*

67 Consider testing accommodations to be sure students have a chance to show what they know. For example, allowing answers to be dictated to them, allowing additional time, reading test to student, accepting short answers or highlighting key directions.

68 Consider behavioral supports such as rest breaks, teaching child how to make friends, functional behavioral analysis and teaching independence skills.

69 Consider the theory of multiple intelligences from Howard Gartner when planning lessons for diverse learners.

Some Activities Under the Eight "Intelligences" Include:

- Linguistic — read about it, write about it, talk about it, and listen to it.
- Logical-Mathematical — quantify it, think critically about it, conceptualize it.
- Visual-Spatial — see it, draw it, visualize it, color it, mind-map it.
- Bodily-Kinesthetic — build it, act it out, touch it, get a gut feeling for it, dance it.
- Musical — sing it, rap it, listen to it.
- Interpersonal — teach it, collaborate on it, interact with respect to it.
- Intrapersonal — connect it to your personal life, make choices with regard to it.
- Naturalist — sense it, feel it, experience it, relate it, think globally about it, be an activist about it.

70 Don't feel like you are taking a disproportionate share of resources when insisting on a quality education for your child. Remember that there are reciprocal benefits of inclusive education. All children benefit from inclusive education.

More Tips to Ensure Access

71 Read the TASH resolution on Inclusive Education. Read it again when you are feeling isolated or tired. Check www.tash.org. Or, choose to write your own resolutions. Read material not only to empower yourself with skills and ammunition, but to edify and motivate you.

72 Consider a dialogue with the administration to support staff training and ongoing professional development opportunities in inclusive education and curriculum modification.

Your success will depend on whether your administration has this kind flexibility built into it.

73 If a paraprofessional is spending some or all of the day with your child, make sure you have built in communication opportunities with him or her. Ask the paraprofessional to write into your child's home/school journal every day. Make sure he or she is invited to team meetings. Insure that training opportunities are made available to him or her.

74 If a paraprofessional is spending some or all of the day with your child, make sure he or she receives ongoing professional development opportunities. Invite them to conferences and seminars. Give them books and literature to read. Make sure they are invited to all of the team meetings and IEP meetings. Have your IEP include training for the paraprofessionals.

Notes: Administrators can support teachers by providing in-service training allow teachers to attend conferences and seminars. Administrators can make sure teachers have time to collaborate with each other and have time to modify and adapt curriculum. Send thank you notes to administrators that support inclusive education. Work with administrators, bringing in-service opportunities to their attention.

75 When planning for an extended school year, do not settle for the "One Size Fits All" program. Consider typical activities with supports and services.

76 Be sure that classrooms have a quiet space for children who need a break from noise and activity. Some ideas for limiting noise include:

- Have a set time for students to use the electric pencil sharpener.
- Use digital timers instead of loud kitchen timers.
- Allow physically active students to kneel or strand by their desks.
- Place easily distracted students near hardworking children in the center of the room.
- Have a quiet corner where students can work and read on beanbags on the floor.

77 If a student needs help with organization, consider the following:

- Allow student to have a second set of books for home.
- Assign a buddy to check if the student turned in homework and reports, and then wrote down the next day's assignments in the student planner.
- Make sure the student has a friend to call if he forgets what HW to do.
- Make sure you own a fax machine so friends can fax assignments.
- Ask that a teacher or teaching assistant meet the student before or after school, or some other, to privately meet with student and help organize his locker one day, and his backpack another day.

78 Transportation is a related service, if a student needs it to access education. It must be looked at carefully. Following are some bus tips.

Notes:

Let's face it; a bus ride is merely 50 unsupervised kids for 10 to 35 minutes. That's a recipe for trouble, even with careful planning. There are no skills to be learned, real people in the real world do not need to learn to ride a bus with 50 kids. Additionally, the bus is where the worst teasing takes place. The truth is, a bus ride is a situation no sane mother ever would voluntarily orchestrate. There is no educational value in a bus ride. The only time an adult will repeat their school bus

Some Bus Tips to Consider

- Give the child an assigned seat near the driver (although the driver keeps his eyes on the road and realistically can't do much supervising).

- Install a camcorder in every bus to see what really goes on. In districts that have done this, incidents have dropped dramatically. Camcorders are really inexpensive these days, so long as they are not digital. It's okay when they break, the kids won't know it.

- Ask the principal to board the bus just before it takes off to "settle" the kids.

- Assign the older students to be bus patrol. It's a privilege for the higher grades. The kids get to wear an orange band across their chest and they rotate turns, one month at a time. If they abuse their responsibilities, they lose the privilege

- Assign a rotating buddy for students who need support.

- Allow students to wear headphones and listen to music if it helps them stay out of trouble.

- Find out, though an auditory evaluation and a sensory integration evaluation, if the bus environment is troubling to the student.

- Change the bus route so a student can have a shorter ride.

- Make sure the bus rules are really clear.

- Ask the bus driver to post the rules in the bus, using pictures as well as words.

- Create social stories (*using Carol Gray's book as a guide — address: Future Horizons, Inc., 721 W. Abram St., Arlington, TX 76013, email: info@futurehorizons-autism.com*) to help deal with bus scenarios

- Consider picking up your child every day from school. You will have important daily contact with the teachers.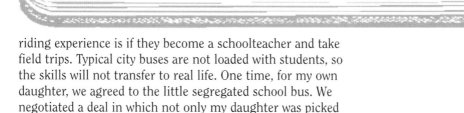

riding experience is if they become a schoolteacher and take field trips. Typical city buses are not loaded with students, so the skills will not transfer to real life. One time, for my own daughter, we agreed to the little segregated school bus. We negotiated a deal in which not only my daughter was picked up, but my sons and all the other children in our cul-de-sac as well. They loved the private service.

— Anne

Notes

Tracking Progress Tips to Monitor the IEP

A common point of friction between schools and families is the question of whether or not a child is making appropriate progress in school. Goals that state that children will "improve their social skills" or "improve their math skills" are wide open to interpretation. How much improvement is enough? What exactly will be improved? How long will we wait before we are satisfied that improvement has occurred? A way to avoid these potentially heated debates is to state goals in measurable terms using every day language and to be sure all members of the team understand how progress will be measured.

Monitoring the IEP is a team effort that includes the parent. Formulate a monitoring strategy. If a student is not making expected progress, then perhaps the teachers need to determine how to improve their instructional effectiveness. Remember, the IEP should change as your child changes.

"The IEP process is long haul. The hard work comes after the IEP meeting."

79 Make sure the IEP contains built in ways to communicate with school staff. For example, ask for scheduled planning time each week so the regular education teachers can plan modifications with the Special Education teachers. You should ask to be allowed to attend those meetings once every 4 to 8 weeks. You can also ask for monthly team meetings to discuss issues and have a communication journal go back and forth each day.

80 Volunteer at the school. Get to know the players. Watch what is going on and develop information sources.

Understand that the modification planning time should not be used to discuss other issues that should be reserved for the monthly team meeting or a separate conference. If curriculum planning does not occur then that week may not be successful.
— Anne

81 Find or cultivate an "inside advocate."

Ideally, one of the members of the IEP team should serve as your "inside" or "school based" advocate. It's often the one professional who seems immune to hidden school agendas and the inflexible nature of a school bureaucracy and thinks about what is best for your child.

My "inside" advocate will remain silent when the school gives me the "party line"; then, after the meeting I will find out what really happened or who was being the gatekeeper. My inside advocates aren't disloyal staff, but professionals who are deeply invested in my child's success and do not fear collaborating with me. Some inside advocates will never openly align themselves with the parent, but they are always watching out for the student.— Anne

82 Seek out information about your child from other parents who may visit the school as well as kids that they see when they go to school. Many children with disabilities — particularly young children — will not be able to give you an accurate report of their day. You may need to be creative to gather information about what is happening with your child at school.

83 Ask school personnel to include your child in monitoring their own progress. For example, if your child is working on improving his reading fluency, he could track his progress on a graph. Visual records of progress allow children to see immediate evidence of their accomplishments and create a data record. There are many computer data entry programs that create colorful graphs (such as Excel). For younger children, charts can be created that look and work like game boards.

"Sometimes there really are real wolves at the door. Sometimes the sky is really falling," says Bob Kafka, ADAPT activist."

84 If possible, avoid the bus and pick up your child everyday.

This tip can really inconvenience your life! I know, I picked up my children for several years, each and every day. Why do I do it? In addition to avoiding bus issues, I was able to have daily contact with the teacher or teaching assistant. Every day I arrived at school 5 minutes before dismissal. My body was always in the same spot. When my kids appeared, I read their faces so I know what kind of day it had been.
— Anne

85 Don't ever trust the school 100%, no matter how nice and caring they are. When things are going well and even if your child is successfully included, it's not time to nap. Stay forever vigilant.

86 Be sure that IEP goals are measurable.

Tips on Writing Measurable Goals

- You shouldn't have to guess how the child's progress is being measured. For example, "Mary will improve in reading" is not measurable. An example of a measurable annual goal would be, "Given 30 minutes of individual instruction in phonological awareness on a daily basis, Mary will progress from a first grade reading level to a second grade reading level as measured by the Degrees of Reading Power (DRP) assessment."

- When percentages are used to report progress, be sure there is enough information to clearly explain what is being measured and how. For example, if you are told that your child forms their letters with 80% accuracy, does that mean that 80% of the time all the letters are formed accurately, or 8 out of 10 letters are formed accurately, or something else entirely?

80%

87 Be sure that measures are objective. It is not helpful to hear that your child is" improving" if you have nothing concrete to refer to. If work samples will be used to assess progress, sit down with the teacher to review exactly how the work is evaluated. For example, are errors counted? Is there a rubric? Is there a point system? And so on.

88 Ask your child's teachers and related service personnel to paraphrase and summarize reports rather than reading them word for word at the IEP meeting. If there is anything in the report that you do not understand, say so. Reports should contain an absolute minimum of jargon. If clinical terms are unavoidable, ask the evaluator to include a written explanation of the unfamiliar term in layman's language.

89 Don't set the bar too low when writing goals. It is common for goals and objectives to target a 70% or 80% success rate but think carefully about how the goal plays out in real life. If a goal states that a child will speak in a respectful tone of voice to adults with 70% accuracy that means that 30% of the time (almost 2 hours out of the school day!) the child is disrespectful.

90 Don't wait for the annual review to assess whether the child is making acceptable progress. With a measurable goal, you will know whether or not the instructional plan is working early enough to make adjustments. For example, if the annual goal states that Chelsea will progress one year in her math skills, and at the first quarter she has made only one month of progress (as measured by an objective assessment tool) then it is clear that the instructional plan does not meet Chelsea's needs and must be amended or fortified. When a child isn't progressing as expected, the approach should be "what can we do differently" NOT the assumption that the child can't achieve the goal.

Chapter 5

On Friendships

True friendship between children with and without disabilities is possible and has been shown to be beneficial to a child's well being. Making sure students with disabilities develop friendships should be among the highest priorities for the IEP team. Many children will require facilitation and support by adults and peers to make and keep friends. School personnel can encourage friendship by insuring that children are fully participating members in all aspects of school life. They can remove barriers, which might include hovering teaching assistants or lack of transportation to after-school events. There should be specific strategies devoted to fostering relationships. Parents can encourage friendship by making sure their children participate and are supported in typical recreational opportunities. Although friendships can't be forced, parents should also encourage relationships that are blossoming.

"Friends are like smakerals of fun. You can never have too many."

Winnie the Pooh

91 The two keys to friendship are close proximity and frequent opportunity to interact. Therefore, make sure your child has close proximity to peers by attending typical classes in your neighborhood school. There is where frequent opportunity to interact will occur.

92 Again, always consider close proximity and frequent opportunity to interact. Enroll your child in typical community activities. If your child needs support, ask that those supports be put into place.

93 Friendships can be better fostered if the teacher uses cooperative learning strategies. Your child can and should be a meaningful member of cooperative groups in school. If kids are pitted against each other in highly competitive activities, then friendship opportunities are lost. When students work together in school, it builds a stronger foundation for developing friendships.

94 The teachers can be key in fostering friendships. They are role models for the other students. They must value each child with or without a disability and respect learning differences. If you notice that the adults in school treat your child in a condescending manner or in a way that is not age-appropriate, ask them to stop.

I attended an IEP meeting with a friend. She shared that recently her 3rd grade daughter with Down syndrome had a play-date. A small squabble occurred, and the visiting friend said, using a kindergarten voice, "If you don't play nicely with me, you won't get your Hershey Kiss as a reward." How telling this was, the young friend was imitating how she saw the teacher treat the student at school. Children notice everything. — Anne

95 Encourage the teachers to find ways to highlight your child's strengths, interests, and talents. If 2 kids love the same baseball team, board game, or they both fish, then there is an increased chance of friendship because they have something in common. Get acquainted activities are a great way to start of the school year. Ask the teacher how the other kids can get to know all about your child's hobbies, interests, and recent vacations or adventures. If a child's hobby or area of expertise is celebrated in class, their status will be elevated.

96 Ask the teacher to infuse ability awareness training in the everyday curriculum. Provide teachers' lists of accomplishments that persons with disabilities have contributed to our society. These lists are readily available on the internet. Make sure that social justice is part of what kids are learning.

97 Ask the teachers which kids seem to be interested and friendly with your child. Then find a way to extend this interest to after school hours. Invite them over or plan an interesting activity and invite them to join you.

98 It's hard to have friends when you can't communicate your ideas using words. Make sure your child has a way of communicating to others. Perhaps some form of assistive technology can give a student a way to communicate. Make sure his or her peers get trained in the technology as well.

Notes:

One of the reasons we got a dog is so others kids would be attracted to our house, and my daughter would have something interesting to talk about. I selected an older dog that was well trained with good manners. I occasionally bring the dog with me when I have to pick up my daughter from an activity. Immediately, the other kids will swarm around us, wanting to pet the dog and asking questions about her. This gives my daughter a lot of positive attention. — Anne

99 Some kids have too many adults surrounding them all day at school. These adults can be barriers to friendships. A teaching assistant should not be Velcroed onto your child or behave like a hovercraft. They are there to facilitate friendships, not to be your child's friend. Make sure that the teaching assistant understands this. In fact, tell her personally.

100 Consider discontinuing the use of a teaching assistant. Often they keep teachers from taking full ownership of the student. They enable the student to rely on someone else instead of becoming independent. Think about all the things that could happen without the assistance of a teaching assistance. Then see how natural supports could take the place of what the teaching assistant was doing.

101 A child will not enjoy academic success if he or she is socially unhappy. Sometimes specific social skills can be taught. Meet with the school team and find out what skills your child might need and if those are skills that can formally be taught. Some skills include being pleasant, turn taking, smiling, giving compliments to others, personal space awareness and being interested in others. These skills do not have to be taught in isolation or in a group with other kids with disabilities. These skills can be part of a lunch bunch with typical peers.

Recently we bought Dance Dance Revolution and Karaoke for our teenagers. Our house has grown five-fold in popularity!
— Anne

102 Make sure your house has up-to-date fun and "cool" things to do, so kids will want to come over to visit. If you have the best toys or latest music, then your house will become a magnet for kids. Be sure that you offer tasty snacks or meals to guests and make them feel welcome. It's okay to get advice from other kids on what is the latest and greatest.

103 Make sure your child dresses appropriately. It's okay to follow fashion fads. If a kid looks cool, other people may jump to the conclusion that she is cool. It's not fair to judge people by their outward appearances, but we do this all the time; make sure your child looks attractive and hip.

Notes: Recently my own daughter, Eva, had a growth spurt so she needed new clothes. Frankly, I didn't know what was stylish so I asked Amy, a neighbor's daughter if she would help us shop. Amy is in the same grade as my daughter and is popular. We went off on a spree. I also bought Amy a few articles of clothing! As a result, not only did we have a great time, but Eva looks good, and Amy is eager to shop again or give us advice whenever we need new clothes.

— Anne

Notes

Chapter 6

Handling Disagreements

As with any close partnership, differences of opinion are inevitable at various points in the IEP process. The law provides legal protections for parents and students, but it is always better to work out disagreements at the building level before a legal path is taken. The members of the IEP team must work to build ways of resolving differences without placing blame and damaging relationships between team members.

"Honest differences are often a healthy sign of progress."

Mahatma Gandhi

Educating parents about the special education process has been shown to reduce conflicts between parents and schools. In studies of conflict resolution in special education, breakdowns of communication between parents and schools were often caused by parents and school district personnel not being adequately informed about the extent and complexity of special education laws and regulations.

"Get to their hearts, not their policy manuals."

Judith Snow, inclusion advocate

104

Know how to handle difficult conversations.

How to Handle Difficult Conversations

- Begin by finding things that you all agree with. **Example:** I know that you have found it hard to teach John because his behavior is challenging at school. I deal with these challenges every day when he comes home and it can be exhausting.

- Use "I" statements in place of "you" statements. "I" statements state how you feel; "you" statements are critical or judgmental. **Example:** Say, "I am feeling that I am not a member of the team because I don't get enough information about what is going on in school" instead of "You never let me know what's going on. Why can't you ever write in our communication journal?"

- Avoid negatives because people will feel hostile. **Example:** Say, "Can we try . . ." or "Is it possible . . ." Don't say, "Why won't you . . ."

- Avoid dictating to the school. **Example:** Say, "Could we consider . . . ?" Don't say, "Stop doing . . . "

- Try to see things from the school's point of view, but don't compromise your principles. In some conflicts, both sides can be right. Ask lots of questions so you can see the advantages of both points of view.

- Find some positive comments to share with the team.

- If you ask a yes or no question, the school might say NO. Instead, start a question with these words — "What would it take in order to . . ." In this way, the school will start brainstorming solutions instead of refusing to do something.

- Try not to yell. In fact, try lowering your voice when you are angry.

105 Distinguish between personal conflicts with staff members and disagreements about your child's education. Sometimes members of the team will disagree, but they are usually focused on what is appropriate for the child. Unfortunately, on rare occasions the school staff is simply rude, tired or simply does not like you or your child. It's always best to try to stay diplomatic and focus on the issues. After all, as attorney Pete Wright says, "Unless you are willing to pay for a private school, your relationship with the school is like a marriage with no possibility for divorce."

106 Put everything in writing. Document all conversations by either keeping contemporaneous records or following up with a letter. Here are two samples of letters you can send to document a conversation.

Dear Teacher,

Thank you very much for meeting with me this morning. You stated that the principal advised you that my son's extended school year might be cut from 6 to 3 weeks based on recent budget concerns. I shared that the IEP team agreed that my son needed a six-week program in order not to further regress in his reading skills. You stated that you would get back to me in the next couple of weeks.

If I have misunderstood our conversation in any way, please advise me in writing within 5 school days.

Thanks,

Savvy Parent

"*No matter how difficult the past, you can always begin again today.*"

Buddha's Little Instruction Book

Dear Teacher,

Thanks for telephoning me today. You were concerned that my son was having a tough time worrying about me since my recent illness. We agreed that we would relax the rule about no cell phones at school and allow Frank to carry one. Let me know if this is what we agreed to.

Thanks so much,

Savvy Parent

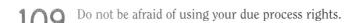

107 Pick your battles. Don't focus on a small mistake or misjudgment. Don't worry about small procedural violations that cause no harm. You can document them, but don't make them an issue.

108 When you are in the teacher's classroom or in an administrator's office, look for any posters or knick-knacks that have a motto or quote on it. Make a note of this motto. When dealing with the person, in an appropriate moment remind them of the motto or quote they chose to display. For example, if the teacher is pushing for another pullout, remind her about the poster that says, "All Kids Belong."

109 Do not be afraid of using your due process rights.

110 Decide ahead of time what is non-negotiable and practice appropriate phrases to state your position. Repeat these phrases over and over each time someone argues or tries to push you to change your mind. If it is critical to your family that your child is in a regular class for all their academic subjects, you might say, "We feel that Steven can be successful in a regular education classroom with appropriate supplementary aids and services." Practice saying this ahead of time and repeat as often as necessary to make it clear that you are not flexible on this point.

111 Practice responses to prepare for what you expect the school-based team to say. Be aware of time honored traditional lines that schools use to control the IEP process and rehearse your responses. Following are some examples;

1. **Principal:** Remember, IDEA is not fully funded. We simply don't have the money to provide the service you are requesting for your daughter."

   Parent: Our responsibility as a team is to fully comply with the law.

2. **Principal:** I'm sorry, we have a policy against this.

   Parent: What policy is that? Please give me a copy of that policy.

3. **Teacher:** The law says that . . .

   Parent: Here is a copy of the law. Please show me where in it says . . .

4. **Special Education Teacher:**
   The teacher is not trained in special education.

   Parent: Inclusion is just good teaching. All teachers should use differentiated instruction to benefit all students. Can I suggest including teacher training in Orville's IEP, since this is a service permitted through IDEA?

"Obstacles are those frightful things you see when you take your eyes off your goals."

Unknown

Principal: I cannot expect my teachers to figure out the best way to teach your daughter in every single situation.

Parent: I'm not expecting her to. This is a team effort. That's why there needs to be adequate paid planning time built into the teacher's schedule.

5. Special Education Teacher: The team feels that . . .

Parent: But I don't feel that way. However, I am willing to compromise and I am a full member of the IEP team.

6. Teacher: You are too personally and emotionally involved to make a reasonable decision.

Parent: Yes, I am very personally involved. That's precisely the reason I have a lot to contribute.

7. Teacher: Your child is not ready to be in the regular classroom all day.

Parent: The law is very clear that my daughter has a right to be in the regular education class and it is our responsibility to design the supports and services she needs to be successful. The law is clear that children don't have to earn the right to be in regular education.

"*. . . I can tell you . . . this: Neither status not wealth matters as much as your support. The simple fact is that you — the parent — are the most powerful advocate your child will ever have.*"

Anne Ford, Chairman, National Center for Learning Disabilities.
Daughter of Henry Ford II

9. Principal: Our budget doesn't allow us to buy . . . for every student.

Parent: But we're not talking about every student, we are only talking about Sally and her individual needs.

10. Special Education Teacher: How do you expect your child to learn Math in the regular classroom?

Parent: If neither of us is sure how to do this, maybe we should get a consultant to help us figure it out.

112 Become efficient in your use of time so you can find the time to train to be an effective advocate for your child.

Anne's Strategies for "Sharpening the Saw"

- I always buy tapes or CDs from conferences that help me understand inclusion, the law, or have advocacy instruction. I play these tapes, sometimes over and over whenever I am driving somewhere, so traveling by car becomes a time to be empowered. Try to upgrade your car stereo so it has the capability to play MP3 format. In this way, several hours of seminars, sometimes the entire conference, can be played from just one MP3 CD. It's less expensive to buy conference CDs this way. Seminars can now be uploaded onto an MP3 player and played back using your car speakers.

- I use these tapes and CDs in a Walkman or attach my iPod to me and play them while doing some tedious or automatic duties such as grocery shopping. Sometimes, if I am watching my children play in the distance, such as sitting on a park bench while they are on the playground equipment, I'll whip out my headphones. It's better than reading a book if you need to keep your eyes on your children. Also, if another Mom sits next to me and starts idle chatter, merely to pass away the time, I simply say, "Sorry to be rude but I am taking a class and I need to hear this lecture before our test this week."

- When a good speaker is presenting, I bring a tape recorder to their seminar. I then listen to the tape, sometimes over and over and over. When you hear an excellent presentation several times, the knowledge stays with you. Also, if there are good "one-liners" and "comebacks," I incorporate that into my personal repertoire.

- I purchase or borrow videotapes and DVDs on disability related topics and watch them while walking on the treadmill. I purchase new tapes, win them on eBay, or borrow them from local disability related organizations.

- When you think of a good idea, write it quickly in your Palm, on your computer, or in a note pad. Have a folder created for good ideas or tips. If that idea comes to you while in the car, have a tiny recorder always handy to speak into.

- I keep books on inclusion on my bathroom counter where I blow dry and curl my hair. I can read while curling. Since the books are so interesting, I give my hair plenty of time to be curled so I not only look good for the day but also I am well informed. I also keep important books next to my bed, so I can read if I can't sleep. Also I keep books in my car so I can read when I am waiting for someone. I have important inclusion tips uploaded onto my Palm so they are always available to read.

- I print important parts of the law on index cards and place them on the mirror and cupboards so they can painlessly be committed to memory.

Notes

Chapter 7

Forming Effective Partnerships Between Families and Schools

Families and schools have a history of functioning autonomously but the education of children with disabilities requires an ongoing, collaborative relationship between home and school. This partnership, which can span 15 years or more, requires a commitment on the part of both systems to share responsibility for the success of the partnership. The benefits of strong family school partnerships cannot be overstated. We have long known that the higher the level of parent involvement, the higher the level of student achievement. Other benefits of strong family-school collaboration include improved student attendance, higher aspirations for postsecondary education and career development, improved social competence and lower rates of high-risk behavior on the part of adolescents. Simply put, when the interests of home and school are shared, successful school experiences and positive outcomes are more likely to occur.

"People who work together will win, whether it be against complex football defenses, or the problems of modern society."

Vince Lombardi, football coach for the NFL (1913-1970)

113 Ask the Director of Special Education how you can volunteer to help her with projects. Find a way that you can work with him or her to make the school a better place for all kids.

114 Start or join a parent group. Make sure there are networking opportunities as well as informational speakers. Create a web site for your parent group so parents know where to go for information.

115 Educate the staff about your child's disability and about your child's needs. Sometimes it appears that the school is refusing to meet your child's needs. In fact, they just don't understand what is needed. You must teach them what you know, based on your unique and rich journey as a parent with a child with a disability.

116 Don't view the school as an enemy. Understand that most teachers want to include your child, they just may not know how. Professor Lou Brown says, "Water professionals and they will grow." We have found that given the opportunity, professionals will rise to the occasion.

117 Write thank you letters. Don't wait until the last day; write them all year long. When a teacher makes extraordinary efforts to include your child, thank them in a letter with a copy to the principal so the letter will go into the personnel file. Let the administration know when staff is doing a good job. Most people respond positively to praise and will work harder and smarter as a result. Thank you letters can also be used as a way to document conversations but should not have a hidden agenda.

118 Find many ways to give positive feedback. If a teacher does something to facilitate an inclusive school community, write a press release and send it to the local newspaper. Then make copies of the article and send it to the teacher as well as the principal. Ask that the story be put in the teacher's file.

Notes:

When I moved into my town, I wrote the special education director a letter introducing myself and asking her if my skills would be of any value to her. I advised her that I was available for projects and committees. I was very clear as to what my vision was, full and successful inclusion for all students with disabilities. I included a business card, which just had everyone's name in my family and our contact information. When I went to see the special education director for the first time, I noticed that my card was tacked onto

119 When you form alliances with school staff, don't forget employees who are not teachers or administrators. It is important to have good relationships with the cafeteria staff, the secretaries, the custodians, the nurse and the playground and bus supervisors. They work hard and they deserve your respect. These people are invaluable to help your child be fully and successfully included. They can make the school a more pleasant and friendly place. They can also be your eyes and ears when you are not in school. Ask them for their opinions; they see everything. Make sure you remember to thank them for their care and services. Notice them, do nice things for them throughout the year.

One time a custodian walked over to me and said how wonderful it was that Eva was going to classes with all the other kids and how different it was when he was a child. He then went on to say that Eva had been happy at the school the last couple of years and that's why he was surprised to find her hiding in his supply closet lately! As it turns out, there were some issues brewing at school that only came to my attention via the custodian.

Another time a mother called the school to report that my daughter was picking her nose on the bus and should not be allowed to ride. The school toyed around with some rules that Eva would have to follow if she wanted to keep her riding privileges. It was the bus driver who intervened and said that most of the kids picked their noses, even more so than Eva and also my daughter was one of the few students who sat safely in her seat.

During middle school, the cashier in the cafeteria was a godsend. I could count on my child being warmly greeted every day. When I occasionally could dropped in for lunch, I learned who had been helpful during lunch and who my daughter sat with.

The stories go on and on, each and every year. I am forever indebted to the band of hard working individuals who answer the phones and clean the schools and serve the lunches at school. — Anne

her small and private bulletin board. I have remained true to my promise. I have volunteered for every possible opportunity. I have approached her with ideas for the school district and offered to do all of the work. I have rescheduled doctor appointments and even vacations just to accommodate her wishes. If I did not agree with or respect the special education director, I would still go out of my way to get on her good side, without compromising my values or philosophy. Fortunately, in my district, I discovered an extremely intelligent and caring individual who was committed to following both the law and best educational practices in our school district.

— Anne

Tips on How to Grow Inclusion Minded Staff

120 Provide books to the teachers on inclusion and other disability related matters. Give books as end of year or holiday gifts instead of gift certificates for a manicure.

121 Make sure each staff member personally hears about training opportunities. If you get a flyer on a seminar or conference, make sure the information is personally put into each team member's hand. Don't just give the school one copy of an upcoming seminar and hope they circulate it. Make several copies and insure that each individual connected with your child gets a copy. Ask them directly if they would be interested in attending. Post flyers on a bulletin board.

122 Make sure the community learns about training opportunities and disability related events. Write press releases about upcoming events and fax or e-mail it to all of the local papers. Buy a fax machine. Create a list of fax numbers of newspapers, advocacy groups, and disability related organizations. Put that list in a protective plastic sleeve, and keep it next to the fax machine at all times. Always pass on information. Everyone needs to be kept in the loop; we need to stand on each others shoulders to create inclusive communities.

123 Don't be afraid to speak up about school district practices that segregate children with disabilities, or portray them in a negative light.

Notes:

When my son was in elementary school, our school district held an annual holiday party at the town hall for children with disabilities. Santa Claus handed out a gift to each "special" child while a photographer took pictures for the local paper.

Ironically, my son was pulled out of his inclusive classroom so he could attend. When I learned that the party was only open to students with disabilities, I denied permission for my son to participate and spent years lobbying for an end to this

124 Create a bulletin board in each school where information about disability related events could be posted for parents and staff to view. Keep it updated. If there are several schools in your district, find someone in each school who can update the bulletin board.

125 Find out how each individual on the team likes to communicate. Some teachers prefer e-mail, others like to speak on the phone in the evening, and some prefer a note. If your child cannot reliably deliver notes via their backpack, consider faxing it. All teachers have mailboxes at school. If you fax a letter, someone in the office will put it in the teacher's mailbox. This method might compromise some privacy, as office staff or parent volunteers could read the letter before it reaches the teacher's mailbox.

126 Learn to use technology to make your advocacy work easier. Start developing lists of contacts that you can quickly and efficiently get information out to. Create a web site just for disability related seminars in your county.

127 As a parent, you can bring new and innovative programs and changes that will impact students and promote inclusion. You are there for the long haul and are deeply invested in the quality of education in your district. You have the time, commitment and energy to overhaul the system. If you remain committed to a vision of fully inclusive schools, you can effectuate change and the administration will be riding on your coattails.

practice. While the intention of the organizers was to do something nice for children, I felt that the event evoked feelings of pity for the "poor disabled children." My son was not happy having to forgo his present from "handicap Santa" and I was very unpopular with the organizers of the event, but in the end many came to see that this type of segregation draws negative rather than positive attention to children with disabilities.
— Kathy

"Only those who attempt the absurd . . . will achieve the impossible."

Anonymous

Notes

I created a web site for my little part of the world. It has grown to become known as "one stop shopping" for people who want to know where to go for local training, how to contact our local resources, and where to find general as well as very local information. Check www.spednet.org to see what was done.

— Anne

Selected by Kathleen Whitbread, Ph.D. & Anne Eason, Esq.

Favorite Websites!

Inclusion Resources:

- ARC United States   www.thearc.org
- Axis Disability Rights   www.normemma.com
- BEACH Center   www.beachcenter.org
- Council for Exceptional Children   www.ideapractices.org
- Disability is Natural   www.disabilityisnatural.com   Read the article on People First Language and share it with everyone you know — especially those who write reports on your child!
- Family Village   www.familyvillage.wisc.edu
- Inclusion Press Homepage   www.inclusion.com
- Kids Together   www.kidstogether.org
- LD Online   www.ldonline.org
- Maryland Coalition for Inclusive Education   www.mcie.org
- NICHCY (National Information Center for Children and Youth with Disabilities) www.nichcy.org
- PACER Center: www.pacer.org
- TASH   www.tash.org
- ThinkCollege.Net   www.thinkcollege.net   A searchable database of college programs and other resources for youth with intellectual disabilities who are considering college
- Universal Design for Learning: CAST   www.cast.org/udl
- Very Special Arts   www.vsarts.org   Check out their Express Diversity program!

Education Law Sites:

- Council of Parent Attorneys and Advocates (COPPA)   www.copaa.org
- Reed Martin   www.reedmartin.com
- WrightsLaw   www.wrightslaw.com

Government Resources:

- ADA Homepage   www.ada.gov
- Family Educational Rights and Privacy Act (FERPA) homepage
  www.ed.gov/policy/gen/guid/fpco/ferpa
- National Technical Assistance Center on Positive Behavioral Interventions and Supports (PBIS). Office of Special Education Programs, US Department of Education   www.pbis.org/main.htm
- No Child Left Behind   www.nochildleftbehind.gov
- US Dept of Education Office of Special Education and Rehabilitative Services (OSERS)   www.ed.gov/about/offices/list/osers

Fun Places to Shop:

- Disability is Natural: www.disabilityisnatural.com/store/index.html

Welcome to the Disability is Natural online store: your source for a variety of products that promote New Ways of Thinking about disability! Great outcomes are possible when we acquire new attitudes and perceptions.

- Human Policy Press: http://thechp.syr.edu/HumanPolicyPress/

Human Policy Press is an independent press, started by the Center on Human Policy in 1974, to promote positive attitudes towards people with disabilities.

- Music From the Heart: www.jeffmoyer.com

Jeff Moyer — Internationally known songsmith, performer, and writer.
Music for all ages — educates, entertains, inspires and unites!

- National Association for Down Syndrome: www.nads.org/pages/pnp.htm

Videos, posters, bookmarks, folders. All related to Down syndrome.

- Nth Degree: www.thenthdegree.com/default.asp

A progressive, forward-thinking graphic design company geared toward issues
related to the independent living movement, inclusion, diversity, and disability rights
movements.

- The Parent Side Online Store: www.cafepress.com/theparentside

It's a campaign for inclusion and against exclusion! Find original unique products that
say it like it is, and let you tell the rest of the world! A wide variety of items
T-shirts, bumper stickers, hats, mugs and more. The perfect gift for an individual with
a disability, their familiy members or any advocate.

- A Positive Perspective: www.apositiveperspective.com

A Positive Perspective offers unique, upbeat designs to help you promote awareness
about Down syndrome and inclusion. A variety of gift and personal items display
positive messages and help create positive perspectives in others.

Our Personal Websites:

Kathy:

- University of Connecticut Center of Excellence in Developmental Disabilities
  (UCEDD): www.uconnucedd.org

Anne:

- Law Offices of Anne I. Eason, LLC: www.spedlawyers.com
- SPED*NET New Canaan: www.spednet.org

Notes